£6.95

Happy walking!

John W Merrill

The John Merrill Foundation & Ministry.
www.johnmerrillwalkguides.com
www.pilgrimways.co.uk

THE LIMEY WAY - 40 MILES
Created and inaugurated by John N. Merrill - May 1969.

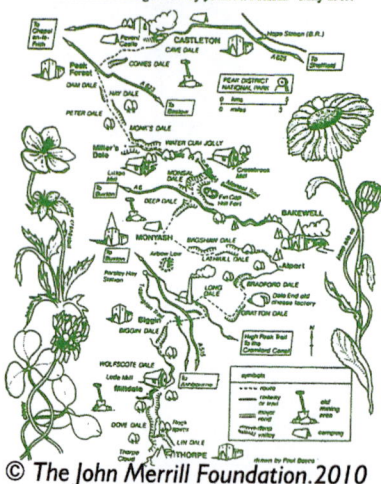

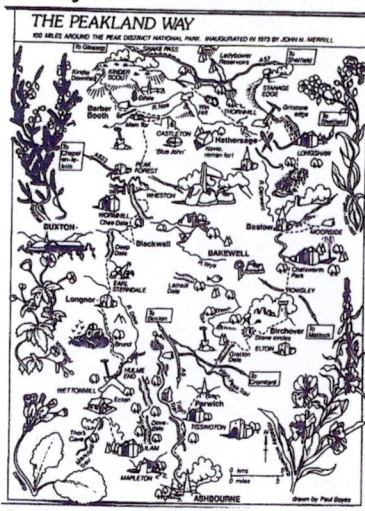

© The John Merrill Foundation. 2010

THE PEAKLAND WAY
100 MILES AROUND THE PEAK DISTRICT NATIONAL PARK. INAUGURATED IN 1973 BY JOHN N. MERRILL

© The John Merrill Foundation. 2010

Walk the finest limestone dale walk in the Peak District -

THE LIMEY WAY

by John N. Merrill
- 40 miles from Castleton to Thorpe via twenty dales. Guide book available from -
THE JOHN MERRILL FOUNDATION

Walk the finest long distant route in the Peak District -

THE PEAKLAND WAY

by John N. Merrill
- 100 mile circular route from Ashbourne taking in the finest places and scenery in the Peak District National Park.

ABOUT THE JOHN MERRILL FOUNDATION

The John Merrill Foundation is a charitable non profit foundation and all profit generated is given to countryside charities, canal societies and footpath preservation societies that the trustees feel are in line with the wishes of John Merrill.

The John Merrill Foundation is not associated or part of any walking organisation and is totally independent in own right.

Happy walking!

John N. Merrill

THE ART OF WALKING THE JOHN MERRILL WAY

1. Always set off in the clothes you plan to wear all day, given the weather conditions. Only on sudden changes in the weather will I stop and put on a waterproof or warmer clothing.

2. Set off at a steady comfortable pace, which you can maintain all day. You should end the walk as fresh as when as you started.

3. Maintain your pace and don t stop. Stopping for any period of time disrupts your rhythm and takes upwards of a mile to settle back down into the flow/ease of movement.

4. Switch off your mobile phone and music centre, and listen and enjoy the countryside - the smells of the flowers, bird song, the rustle of the leaves and the tinkling stream.

5. Ignore the mileage and ascents - don t tick off the miles, just concentrate on what the walk s goal is. To think otherwise slows you down and makes the walk a struggle rather than a joy. In a similar vein, when ascending just keep a steady pace and keep going. To stop is to disrupt the flow and make the ascent interminable.

6. Whilst a walk is a challenge to complete, it is not just exercise. You should enjoy the world around you; the flowers, birds, wildlife and nature and look at and explore the historical buildings and church s that you pass. All are part of life s rich tapestry.

7. Remember that for every mile that you walk, you extend your life by 21 minutes.

8. A journey of a 1,000 miles begins with a single step and a mile requires 2,000 strides.

The expert traveller
leaves no footprints.
Lao Tzu.

THE BELVOIR WITCHES CHALLENGE WALK

by John N. Merrill

Maps, pencil sketches and photographs by John N. Merrill

"I hike the paths and trails of the world for others to enjoy."

© John N. Merrill 2011

THE JOHN MERRILL FOUNDATION

The Day Challenge Walk Series.

2011

THE JOHN MERRILL FOUNDATION
32, Holmesdale, Waltham Cross, Hertfordshire, England. EN8 8QY

Tel/Fax - 01992-762776
E-mail - marathonhiker@aol.com
www.johnmerrillwalkguides.com
www.pilgrimways.co.uk

International Copyright © John N. Merrill. All rights reserved. No part of this publication may be reproduced or transmitted in any form or by any means electronic or mechanical including photocopy, recording or any information storage or retrieval system in any place, in any country without the prior written permission of The John Merrill Foundation.

John N. Merrill asserts the moral right to be identified as the author of this work.

A catalogue record for this book is available from the British Library.

Typeset and designed by *The John Merrill Foundation*
Printed and handmade by *John N. Merrill.*
Book layout and cover design by *John N. Merrill*

©Text and photographs - by John N. Merrill, HonMUniv, 2009.
© Maps, sketches & paintings, by John N. Merrill, HonMUniv, 2009.

ISBN 978-1-903627-59-4
First published - October 2004. Revised and enlarged - May 2009
Special limited edition.

Typeset in Humanst521 - bold, italic, and plain 11pt, 14pt and 18pt
Main titles in 18pt .**Humanst521 Bd BT** by John Merrill in Adobe Pagemaker on a iMac.

Please note - *The maps in this guide are purely illustrative. You are encouraged to use the appropriate 1:25,000 O.S. Explorer map as detailed on each walk.*

John Merrill confirms he has walked all the routes in this book and detailed what he found. Meticulous research has been undertaken to ensure that this publication is highly accurate at the time of going to press. The publishers, however, cannot be held responsible for alterations, errors, omissions, or for changes in details given. They would welcome information to help keep the book up to date.

Cover design and photographs - Belvoir Castle - by John N. Merrill
© The John Merrill Foundation 2009.

Printed on paper from a 100% sustainable forest.
The John Merrill Foundation plants sufficient trees through the Woodland Trust to replenish the trees used in its publications.

The author near Tower Bridge with his medal, after completing Walk for Life, a charity walk in June 2009.

ABOUT THE AUTHOR

Over the last 40 years John Merrill has walked over 200,000 miles, - more than ten times around the world - wearing out 108 pairs of boots in the process. He has completed a remarkable and unequalled number of marathon walks - walking more than 28 miles per day on average - including being the first person to walk around Britain - 7,000 miles - in ten months. He has walked across Europe, Africa, India, Nepal, Asia, America, and along the great trails of America and Canada. He has completed numerous Pilgrim routes to Santiago de Compostela, Canterbury, Walsingham, St. Albans and to Trondheim in Norway. Many more pilgrimages and marathons are planned.

He has written more than 320 guidebooks to his walks, most of which he prints and publishes himself. After his coast walk he realised the fame game prevented his from doing what he was destined to do, and that was to simply walk and write. He purposefully left the stage and concentrated on what he wanted to do. He does not consult anyone, promote or seek publicity; preferring to follow his own quiet spiritual path through life. This means he can write a book, on average one every month. He is not beholden to anyone, just a free spirit, with no staff, agents or editors. As a result he is not rich in money terms but in life and places walked to, a millionaire.

He is not a loner, quite the reverse, but to get the material and accomplish his walks - he who travels alone, travels fastest. And, by going alone you never forget. He is guided and has a very deep spiritual faith and has never come to any harm or put a foot wrong. The only way to be close to nature and see its huge variety is by walking; no other sport/exercise gives you that connectedness to the earth. He does no research beforehand, preferring to walk around the corner and come to a church, historic house, sacred site etc., and discover for himself their secrets. To be aware of what's next is to dampen the impact.

" A journey of a thousand miles, begins with a single step."
Lao Tzu (The Tao Te Ching).

I am on a long journey, which continues daily - one life is not enough.

"Do not seek fame.
Do not make plans.
Do not be absorbed by activities.
Do not think that you know.
Be aware of all that is and dwell in the infinite.
Wander where there is no path.
Be all that heaven gave you, but act as though you have received nothing.
Be empty, that is all."

Chuang Tzu

Contents

Page No.

Introduction..7
How to do it...8
About the Walk..9
The Belvoir Witches...10

The Walk -

Stage One -
Bottesford to Muston Bridge 2 1/2 miles..........................12

Stage Two -
Muston Bridge to Harlaxton Bridge - 5 miles...................16

Stage Three -
Harlaxton Bridge to Woolsthorpe by Belvoir - 4 1/2 miles.....20

Stage Four -
Woolsthorpe by Belvoir to Plungar - 7 1/2 miles -.............24

Stage Five -
Plungar to Bottesford - 5 1/2 miles....................................28

Log..32
Badge Order Form..33
Amenities Guide..34
Other John Merrill Day Challenge Walks.........................35
Observe the Country Code..38
Equipment Notes...39
My Walking Philosophy..40
Other Books by John N. Merrill...42

5

The Witches tomb in Bottesford church; note the children carrying skulls.

INTRODUCTION

For many years I have frequently been walking the line of the Grantham Canal for a book in my Canal series. I started from the River Trent in Nottingham slowly completing circular walks, linking the canal. In time as I neared Grantham, the majestic shape of Belvoir Castle dominated the skyline. Years before, I wrote a book on the Folklore of the Midlands and included the story of the Belvoir Witches. Then, quite by chance I went to Woolsthorpe beneath Belvoir Castle and was immediately struck at the sheer beauty of the area. The result, as they say, is this Book!

Drawing on my favourite places - the Canal, Woolsthorpe, the Castle, Denton Reservoir, I hatched the plan to make a challenge walk here, with the Witches history adding spice to the walk. It may not be one of my more "challenging" walks but you still have to walk 25 miles through exceptional scenery, making a hard but very enjoyable day.

I took eight hours for the walk but you can spend longer by exploring the Castle and Bottesford. Starting from Bottesford where many of the Rutland family are buried - there is a three tier tomb in the Church is named the three Witches - you pass through a couple of villages before gaining the Grantham Canal. Five miles of walking past the Woolsthorpe flight of locks you leave the Canal to walk past the delightful Denton Reservoir to Denton and onto the beautiful horse chestnut lined track - Sewstern Lane. From Brewers Gate you emerge from woodland and the stunning view to Belvoir Castle unfolds. You descend to Woolsthorpe by Belvoir and ascend to the Castle. The view from the Castle over the Vale of Belvoir can only be described as breathtaking. Here you enter majestic woodland with huge beech trees, before descending back to the Canal at Plungar. The final miles are along a remote section of Canal before gaining the road back into Bottesford.

Regaining Bottesford with its Church, Stocks and Pillory, I felt sad but elated at such a rewarding walk in the Vale of Belvoir. I hope you have an enjoyable walk as you see some of England's finest and unspoilt scenery. Let me know how you got on!

HOW TO DO IT

The whole walk is covered by the following O.S. 1:50,000 Explorer Series-
No 260 - Nottingham & Vale of Belvoir.
No 247 - Grantham, Bottesford & Colsterworth.

The walk is designed to be done in a day - 8 to 12 hours - longer if visiting Belvoir Castle. There is no time limit and you can do the walk over a weekend and either stay at bed & breakfast establishment or camp at Woolsthorpe Wharf (Rutland Arms); just off the route and approximately at the half way point. Apart from several Inns about five miles apart on the route there are no other facilities. Ice cream is available at Belvoir Castle during the season. Bottesford has shops and a free car park.

Bottesford Car Park - Reached from the High Street via Albert Street and Walford Close and is adjacent to the surgery.

Support parties can link in with the walkers at Muston Bridge on the Grantham Canal; The Rutland Arms at Woolsthorpe Bridge; Harlaxton Bridge at the end of the first canal section; Denton; Woolsthorpe by Belvoir; Belvoir Castle; Plungar and Bottesford.

The route follows well defined paths much of the way with a little road walking to link the whole route together. On the Canal you join a segment of The Viking Way and around Woolsthorpe and Belvoir Castle, a section of the Jubilee Way. Apart from the gentle ascent to Belvoir Castle and short steep descent from the Terrace Hills to Plungar, the walk is basically level.

The successful can obtain a Witches Badge and Completion Certificate as detailed towards the end of the Book.

ABOUT THE WALK
- some general comments.

Whilst every care is taken detailing and describing the walks in this book, it should be borne in mind that the countryside changes by the seasons and the work of man. I have described the walk to the best of my ability, detailing what I have found actually on the walk in the way of stiles and signs. Obviously with the passage of time stiles become broken or replaced by a ladder stile, a small gate or a kissing gate. Signs too have a habit of being broken or pushed over - vandalism. All the route follow rights of way and only on rare occasions will you have to overcome obstacles in its path, such as a blown down tree, barbed wire fence or an electric fence. On rare occasions rights of way are rerouted and these ammendments are included in the next edition. Inns have a frustrating habit of changing their name, then back to the original one!

All rights of way have colour coded arrows; on marker posts, stiles/gates and trees; these help you to show the direction of the right of way.

Yellow - Public footpath.
Blue - Public bridleway.
Red - Byway open to all traffic (BOAT).
Black - Road used as a public path (RUPP).
White - Concessionary and Permissive path

The seasons bring occasional problems whilst out walking which should also be borne in mind. In the height of summer paths become overgrown and you may have to fight your way through in a few places. In low lying areas the fields are often full of crops, and although the pathline goes straight across it may be more practical to walk round the field edge to get to the next stile or gate. In summer the ground is generally dry but in autumn and winter, especially because of our climate, the surface can be decidedly wet and slippery; sometimes even gluttonous mud!

These comments are part of countryside walking which help to make your walk more interesting or briefly frustrating. Standing in a track up to your ankles in mud might not be funny at the time but upon reflection was one of the highlights of the walk!

The mileage for each section is based on three calculations -

1. pedometer reading.
2. the route map measured on the map.
3. the time I took for the walk.

I believe the figure stated for each section to be very accurate but we all walk differently and not always in a straight line! The time allowed for each section is on the generous side and does not include pub stops etc. The figure is based on the fact that on average a person walks 2 1/2 miles an hour but less in hilly terrain. Allow 20 minutes to walk a mile; ten minutes for 1/2 mile and five minutes for 1/4 mile. On average you will walk 2,000 strides to a mile - an average stride is 31 inches..

"For every mile you walk, you extend your life by 21 minutes"

THE
WONDERFVL
DISCOVERIE OF THE
Witchcrafts of *Margaret* and *Phillip Flower*, daughters of *Joan Flower* neere *Beuer Castle:* executed at Lincolne, March 11. 1618.

Who were specially arraigned & condemned before Sir *Henry Hobart*, and Sir *Edward Bromley*, Judges of Assize, for confessing themselues actors in the destruction of *Henry*, Lord *Rosse*, with their damnable practises against others the Children of the Right Honourable FRANCIS Earle of *Rutland*.

Together with the seuerall Examinations and Confessions of *Anne Baker*, *Ioan Willimot*, and *Ellen Greene*, Witches in *Leicestershire*.

Printed at London by *G. Eld* for *I. Barnes*, dwelling in the long Walke neere Christ-Church. 1619.

THE STORY OF THE BELVOIR WITCHES

In the early 1600's, working as charwomen for the Earl of Rutland, at Belvoir Castle, were Joan Flower and her two daughters. One of the daughters, Margaret, was responsible for *"the poultrey abroad and the washhouse within dores."* She was not very good at this and the Countess of Rutland was forever reprimanding her. The trouble reached a peak, and Joan Flower and her daughters were dismissed from the Castle.

Furious at what they thought unfair treatment, they turned to witchcraft to gain their revenge. it is from their trial, years later, that we can piece together the story. Joan Flower was *"a monstrous malicious woman, full of oaths, curses and imprecations irreligious."* Her neighbours *"dared to affirme that she dealt with familiar spirits and terrified them all the curses and threatening of revenge."* Using her cat Rutterkin, Margaret Flower stole a glove belonging to Lord Rosse, the heir to the Earl of Rutland. Her mother stroked the cat with it, then dipped the glove in boiling water, pricked it, and buried it. Lord Rosse later fell ill and died. He was buried at Bottesford, in the Vale of Belvoir, on 26th September 1613.

At this stage, no one suspected that the death was due to witchcraft. Together, mother and daughter cast other spells, which caused the deaths of the second son and daughter of the Earl. To prevent the Earl and Countess from having any more children, three other witches were recruited to weave a spell. They were Anne Baker of Bottesford, Joan Willimot of Goodby and Ellen Greene of Strathorne. Using a pair of gloves and some feathers from the Earls bed, they boiled them in water mixed with blood.

Local gossip about the Flower family increased and the Earl and Countess became suspicious. Early in 1619, the Flowers were arrested. They were taken to Lincoln, but on the way Joan Flower died. She refused to admit anything, *"called for bread and butter, and wished it might never goe through her if she was guilty of that whereupon she was examined"*. With bread in her mouth she *"never spoke more words after, but fell downe and dyed as she was carried to Lincolne Jaile."* Her daughters, Margaret and Phillippa, confessed and were burnt in Lincoln on 11th March 1619.

BOTTESFORD TO MUSTON BRIDGE - 2 1/2 MILES

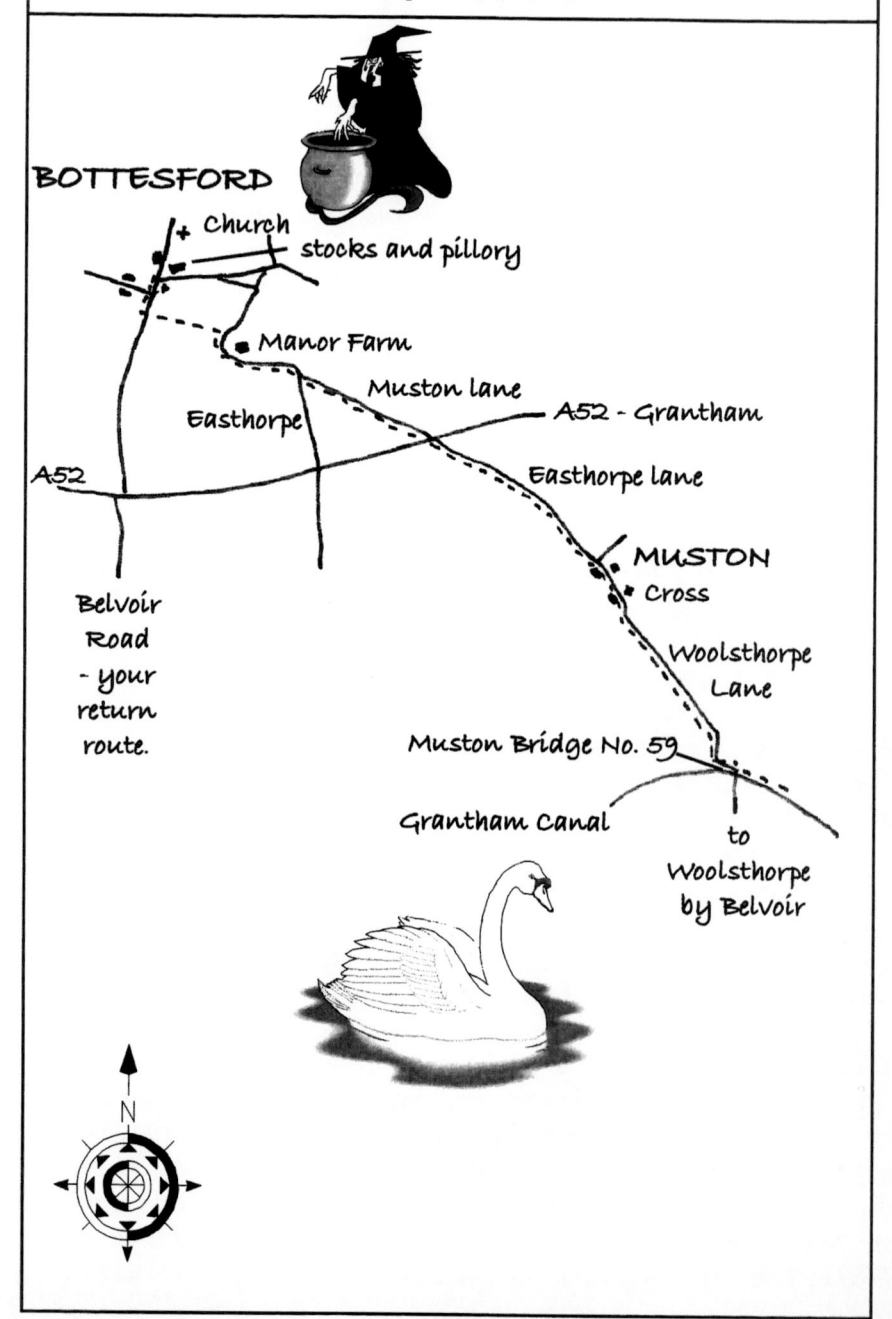

BOTTESFORD
- Church
- stocks and pillory
- Manor Farm
- Easthorpe
- Muston Lane
- A52 – Grantham
- A52
- Easthorpe Lane
- Belvoir Road – your return route.
- MUSTON Cross
- Woolsthorpe Lane
- Muston Bridge No. 59
- Grantham Canal
- to Woolsthorpe by Belvoir

12

Stage One
BOTTESFORD TO MUSTON BRIDGE
2 1/2 Miles
- Allow 50 mins.

Basic route - Bottesford - Manor farm - Muston Lane - Easthorpe Lane - Muston Cross - Woolsthorpe lane - Muston Bridge - Grantham Canal.

O.S. Map - 1:25,000 Explorer Series Sheet No. 247 - Grantham, Bottesford & Colsterworth.

ABOUT THE STAGE - Road and lane walking to the Grantham Canal. A visit to the Bottesford Church is recommended to see the tombs to the Rutland family and "Three Witches" tomb. Closeby at the road junction to the Church are the stocks and pillory post. In the village of Muston you walk past an ancient cross.

WALKING INSTRUCTIONS - From the car park exit via the top righthand corner along a tarmaced path to the High Street and National Westminster Bank. Turn left and pass the Rutland Arms and onto the road junction, with Belvoir Road to your right - you will return along this road. To your left is the way to the Church, stocks and pillory. Turn right along Belvoir Road for a few yards before turning left along the lane to the Village Hall. Continue past the Hall on a tarmaced path and in 1/4 mile reach a kissing gate and Manor road near Manor Farm. Turn right along Manor Road towards Easthorpe and in 1/4 mile turn left along Muston Lane, a No Through Road. Follow this to a stile and A52 Road. Cross over with care, to another stile and lane - Easthorpe Lane - and follow this into Muston village. Keep straight ahead through the village and pass the cross, on your left, now walking along Woolsthorpe Lane. More than 1/2 mile from the village reach Muston Bridge (No. 59) and the Grantham Canal.

BOTTESFORD CHURCH, dedicated to St. Mary. Dates from the 12th. century and is one of the largest village churches in England. The spire rises to 210 ft (64m). Much of the chancel is covered by various tombs of the Rutland family of nearby Belvoir Castle. The "Witches tomb", is top right. The first monument to the first Earl of Rutland, cost at the time £20.

PILLORY AND STOCKS - beside the market Cross stump in Bottesford. Generally the poor occupant had his hands clasped in the pillory for an hour on Market Day. In the stocks only your feet were clasped. The occupant was subject to abuse, often eggs and rotten vegetables were thrown and sometimes stones, resulting in death. This form of punishment was abolished in 1837.

Muston Cross.

MUSTON BRIDGE TO HARLAXTON BRIDGE - 5 MILES

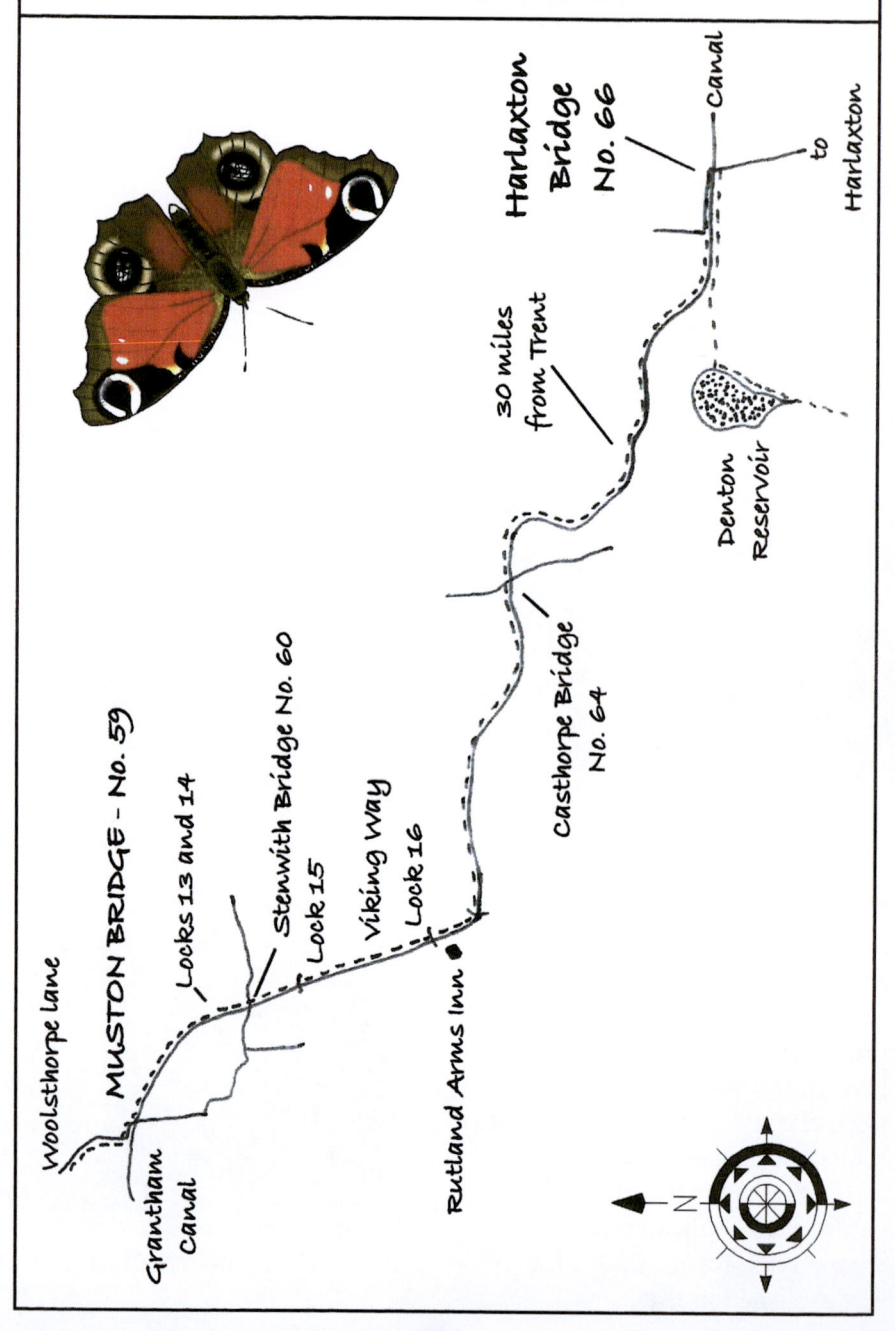

Stage Two
MUSTON BRIDGE TO HARLAXTON BRIDGE VIA THE GRANTHAM CANAL
5 miles - allow 2 hours.

Basic Route - Muston Bridge No. 59 - Grantham Canal - Harlaxton Bridge No. 66.

O.S. Map 1:25,000 Explorer Series Sheet No 247 - Grantham, Bottesford and Colsterworth.

Inns - Rutland Arms Inn, Woolsthorpe Bridge No. 61.

ABOUT THE STAGE - The entire stage is along the towpath of the Grantham Canal. At first you walk past the locks of the Woolsthorpe Flight., which have been restored. The Rutland Arms Inn and campsite is on the other side of the Canal at Woolsthorpe Bridge No.61. You have great views to Belvoir Castle; you have a good 8 miles of walking to get there! You will no doubt see swans, coots, moorhens and Canada geese on the Canal. Sections are popular with Fishermen and there are many 12" long fish to be seen, notably Tench, Perch and Roach. The section ends at Harlaxton Bridge No. 66 - 31 miles from the River Trent.

WALKING INSTRUCTIONS - Gaining the canal at Muston Bridge, No. 50, follow the towpath with the canal on your right and pass a ruined lock. Continue past further locks part of the Woolsthorpe Flight and part of the Viking Way. Pass the Rutland Arms Inn and Top Lock after nearly 2 miles. In a further 2 miles pass Denton Wharf and boat slipway close to Denton Bridge, No.65. Continue a further mile to Harlaxton Bridge No.66, where you ascend to the road.

Grantham Canal at the Rutland Arms Inn, Woolsthorpe.

THE GRANTHAM CANAL - In November 1791 the capital - £40,000 - was raised at a single meeting for the construction of the canal from the River Trent at Nottingham to Grantham. The canal was a useful waterway last century but like so many suffered badly from rail competition. In 1905 18,802 tons were carried and by 1924 this had dwindled to 1,583 tons. Five years later in 1929 it was closed. Today it is sadly derelict with many bridges now gone; sections without water and badly overgrown; and other sections are particularly attractive as this stage shows. The Grantham Canal Restoration Society have placed information plaques where the road crosses the canal. Many sections of the canal are being restored and upper three locks of the Woolsthorpe Flight have in 1994 been restored. Mile posts beside the towpath - they are every 1/4 mile - tell you how many miles you are from the River Trent in Nottingham; the canals start. For a complete guide to walks on the canal see my Grantham Canal guide!

Lock 15 on the Grantham Canal.

Rutland Arms Inn and Grantham Canal.

HARLAXTON BRIDGE TO WOOLSTHORPE BY BELVOIR - 4 1/2 MILES

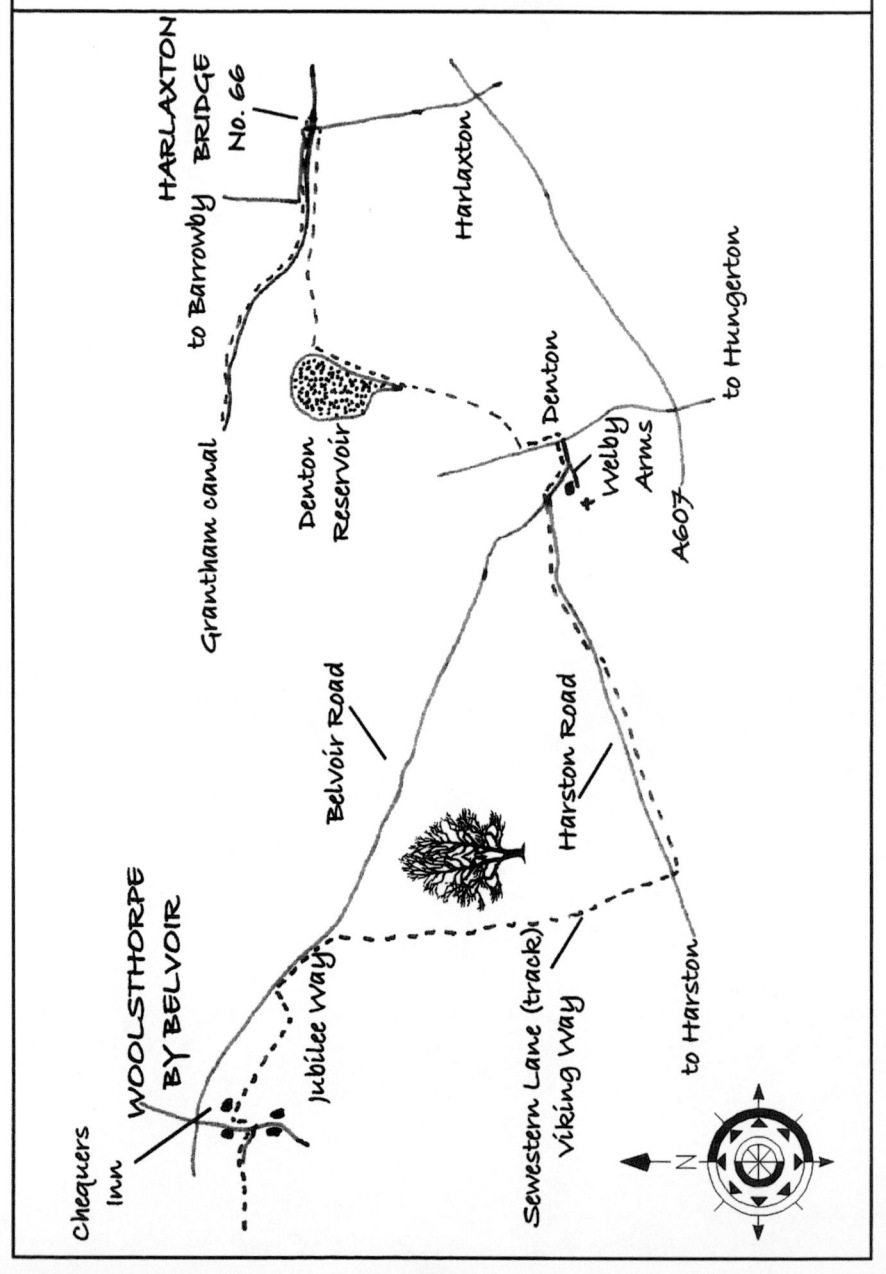

Stage Three
HARLAXTON BRIDGE TO WOOLSTHORPE BY BELVOIR
- 4 1/2 miles
- allow 1 1/2 hours.

Basic Route - Harlaxton Bridge No. 66 - Denton Reservoir - Denton - Harston Road - Sewstern Lane (track) - Viking Way - Jubilee Way - Woolsthorpe by Belvoir.

O.S. Map 1:25,000 Explorer Series Sheet No. 247 - Grantham, Bottesford & Colsterworth.

Inns - Welby Arms, Denton, Chequers Inn, Woolsthorpe by Belvoir.

ABOUT THE STAGE - Leaving the Canal you gain Denton Reservoir feeder reservoir for the Grantham Canal. The scenery here is most attractive. You walk through the village of Denton and by the Harston Road to Sewstern Lane (track). Following the track, another part of the The Viking Way, you join the Jubilee Way and descend with views of Belvoir Castle to Woolsthorpe by Belvoir, nearly halfway on the walk!

WALKING INSTRUCTIONS - From the road at Harlaxton Bridge, No. 66, cross the bridge and turn right along a path to steps and a stile. For the next 1/2 mile you basically walk back above the canal along the righthand side of the field using stiles. Where the canal turns right keep to the lefthand side of the field, beside the hedge, leaving the canal and heading for a stile and footbridge. Cross this continue to another stile and steps and ascend to the wooded fringe of Denton Reservoir. Turn left around the reservoir, crossing footbridges and leave the reservoir by continuing on a defined path, with a stream on your left, to stiles and an old railway line. Cross this and continue to another stile and onto a gate by a footpath sign and road - Casthorpe Road. Turn left into Denton village and turn along Belvoir Road passing the road to the Church, Welby Arms to your right. Soon afterwards turn left along Harston Road.

Pass the Saw Mill on your right and 1/4 mile later the gates to Denton Manor. Here you can leave the road and walk along the righthand side of the fields, or continue along the road for another 3/4 mile to The Viking Way and Sewstern Lane. Turn right along the lane past New Cottages and Socketwell Plantation. The lane now becomes a delightful track with walnut and horse chestnut trees. Little over a mile along the lane reach the road - Cliff Road - at Brewer's Grave. Turn left along the road for 1/4 mile to stile, track and footpath on your left, just before the road descends. Turn left along the track through Fanny's Wood and turn left to its edge to a stile. Turn right and soon start descending as the view over Woolsthorpe by Belvoir to Belvoir Castle unfolds. Descend to a stile by a cricket pitch and walk along its lefthand side to the Chequers Inn and reach the road in Woolsthorpe by Belvoir.

THE VIKING WAY - 140 mile long recreational path from Barton-on Humber, South Humberside, across Lincolnshire to Oakham, Leicestershire. The route is waymarked by a black Viking helmet on a yellow background.

THE JUBILEE WAY - 17 1/2 miles from Melton Mowbray Museum to Brewers Grave near Woolsthorpe; where it meets the Viking Way. Developed by the Leicestershire County Council. The route is waymarked with an orb and crown motif.

BELVOIR CASTLE - The home of the Duke of Rutland whose Peak District home is the renowned medieval Haddon Hall. The Belvoir means beautiful view and the view from the castle area, over the Vale of Belvoir, is one of the finest in England. The original castle was built in Norman times by Robert de Todeni, Standard bearer to William the Conqueror. Today's building is mostly after 1816 when the castle was badly destroyed by fire. The interior has impressive State rooms and is renowned for its collection of art, tapestries, furniture and porcelain. The Queen's Royal Lancers Museum is situated in the castle. Open daily from April to end of September, except Mondays.

Denton Reservoir.

The start of the descent to Woolsthorpe by Belvoir with Belvoir Castle in the distance.

WOOLSTHORPE BY BELVOIR TO PLUNGAR - 7 1/2 MILES

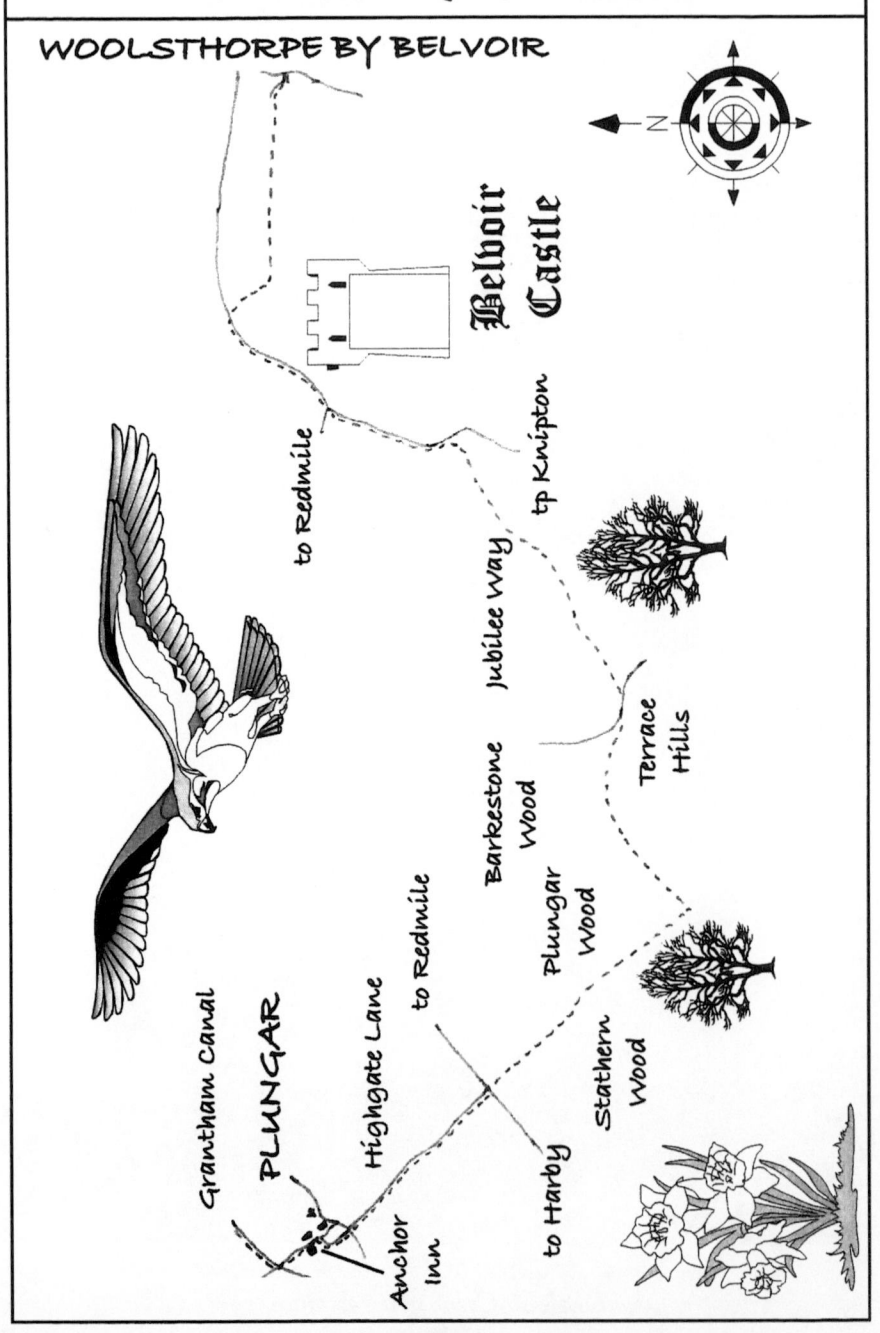

WOOLSTHORPE BY BELVOIR

Belvoir Castle

to Redmile

to Knipton

Jubilee Way

Barkestone Wood

Terrace Hills

Plungar Wood

Statherń Wood

Grantham Canal

PLUNGAR

Highgate Lane

to Redmile

Anchor Inn

to Harby

24

STAGE FOUR WOOLSTHORPE BY BELVOIR TO PLUNGAR - 7 1/2 miles - allow 3 hours.

Basic Route - Woolsthorpe by Belvoir - Belvoir Castle - Old Park Wood - Jubilee Way - Reeded Cottage - Terrace Hills - Plungar Wood - Highgate lane - Plungar.

O.S. Maps 1:25,000 Explorer Sheets Nos.
- 247 - Grantham, Bottesford and Colsterworth.
- 260 - Nottingham & Vale of Belvoir.

Inns - The Anchor Inn, Plungar.
Ice Cream at Belvoir Castle car park during season.
Cafe in Castle.

ABOUT THE STAGE - First you ascend to Belvoir Castle before walking through the woodland of the Terrace Hills, part of the Jubilee Way. Four miles from the Castle you descend steeply at first through woodland to reach the road to Plungar and the final stage of the route!

WALKING INSTRUCTIONS - Gaining the road in Woolsthorpe by Belvoir turn left and in a few yards right down Belvoir Lane. Follow it to its end to a bridge over the River Devon. Ascend keeping the righthand side of the field, following a line of oaks trees, and heading towards the Castle. After nearly a mile turn right as signed and stiled to the road and turn left along it to the Castle car park. Continue along the road beside the woodland for a further 3/4 mile from the Castle to a track, signposted Jubilee Way to Terrace Hills - 1 1/4 miles. The path/track is well defined as you ascend then descend past Old Park Wood on your right to Reeded

Cottage. Continue ahead to a stile and on the track through the woodland past many splendid beech trees. 3/4 mile from the cottage gain a road at Terrace Hills and turn left and in a few yards turn right to continue on the track through the woodland. After a further 3/4 mile gain a wooden hut on your right and pheasant enclosure on your left. Just beyond is a yellow topped post. Here turn right and descend steeply to an opening. Here turn right then left, as signed and keep straight ahead on a 'track', ignoring all turnings. Eventually in 1/2 mile emerging into open fields. Continue straight ahead along the lefthand side of the fields to the road 1/2 mile away. Turn right then left along the road to Plungar 1 mile. The sign says Bottesford is 5 miles away but you have further than that to go! Walk along Highgate Lane to Plungar and where the road turns sharp right continue ahead on Frog Lane. Then turn right down The Gas and into Post Office Lane and the road with the Belvoir on your right. Turn left, pass the Anchor Inn, and in 1/4 mile along here you are back at the Grantham Canal at Bridge No. 49.

Ascending towards Belvoir Castle.

Belvoir Castle.

PLUNGAR TO BOTTESFORD
- 5 1/2 MILES

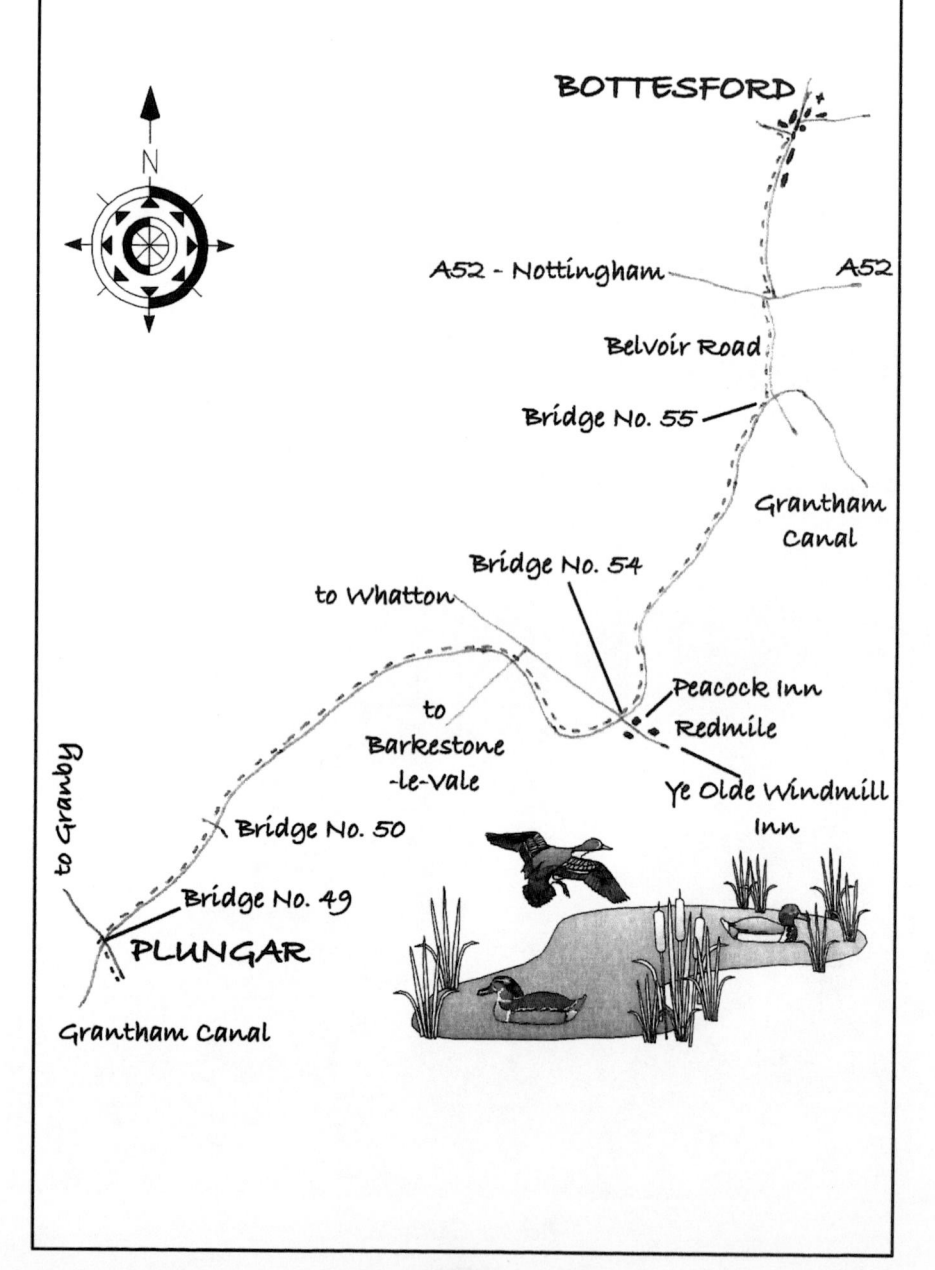

BOTTESFORD

A52 - Nottingham

A52

Belvoir Road

Bridge No. 55

Grantham Canal

Bridge No. 54

to Whatton

Peacock Inn

to Barkestone-le-Vale

Redmile

Ye Olde Windmill Inn

Bridge No. 50

to Granby

Bridge No. 49

PLUNGAR

Grantham Canal

STAGE FIVE
PLUNGAR TO
BOTTESFORD
- 5 1/2 miles
- allow 2 hours.

Basic Route - Plungar - Canal Bridge No. 49 - Grantham Canal - Canal Bridge No. 55 - Belvoir Road - Bottesford.

O.S. Map - 1:25,000 Explorer Sheet No. 260 - Nottingham & Vale of Belvoir.

Inns - Peacock Inn, Ye Olde Windmill Inn, Redmile. Rutland Arms, Bottesford.

ABOUT THE STAGE - Four miles of walking along a remote, quit and delightful section of the Grantham Canal before gaining the road close to where Bottesford Wharf was. From here the final mile back into Bottesford begins. The last Inn of the walk is at Redmile, 3 miles from Plungar and 2 1/2 miles from Bottesford.

WALKING INSTRUCTIONS - Gaining the canal turn right along it along the towpath with the canal on your right. In 1/2 mile pass the milepost - 21 miles from the River Trent. Pass Bridge No. 51 and 1 3/4 miles later reach Bridge No. 54 at Redmile; the Peacock Inn is to your right. Continue beside the canal for another 1 1/2 miles to the site of Bottesford Wharf and Bridge No 55. Gaining the road here turn left down Belvoir Road to the A52 road. Cross over and continue along Belvoir Road into Bottesford passing your early path to the Village Hall on your right. Just after turn left past the Rutland Arms to the National Westminster Bank and turn right back into the car park.

Alas here the walk ends but I hope you enjoyed it! ......***Happy Walking!***

The tranquil Grantham Canal.

Cross base in Bottesford with the spire of the church beyond.

LOG

Date..

Time started .... Time completed ....

Route point	Mile No.	Time	Comments
Bottesford..................	0		
Easthorpe..................	1		
Muston..................	2		
Muston Bridge..........	2 1/2		
Stenwith Lock..........	3		
The Viking Way........	4		
Top Lock..................	5		
Denton Wharf..........	6		
Harlaxton Bridge......	7		
Denton Reservoir......	8		
Denton..................	8 1/2		
Sewstern Lane..........	10		
Jubilee Way..............	11		
Woolsthorpe by Belvoir.	11 1/2		
Belvoir Castle..........	13		
Old Park Wood........	14		
Barkestone Wood......	16		
Highgate Lane........	18		
Plungar..................	18 1/2		
Grantham Canal......	19		
Redmile..................	21 1/2		
Bridge No. 55..........	23 1/2		
Bottesford..............	25		

THE BELVOIR WITCHES CHALLENGE WALK BADGE

Complete the walk in this book and get the above special embroidered badge and signed certificate. Badges are white cloth with witch embroidered in black and red lettering.

BADGE ORDER FORM

Date walk completed..

NAME ....

ADDRESS ....

....

Price: £6.00 each including postage, packing, VAT and signed completion certificate. Amount enclosed (Payable to The John Merrill Foundation) ..

From:
The John Merrill Foundation,
32, Holmesdale,
Waltham Cross,
Herts.
EN8 8QY

Fax +44(0)870 131 5061
e-mail - marathonhiker@aol.com
********** YOU MAY PHOTOCOPY THIS FORM **********

AMENITIES GUIDE

There are few amenities on the route and apart from Inns passed you will have to carry what you need. Grantham is only a few miles from the walk with Nottingham a little further.

INNS
Rutland Arms, Bottesford
Rutland Arms Inn, by Grantham canal north of Woolsthorpe by Belvoir.
The Welby Arms, Denton.
Chequers Inn, Woolsthorpe by Belvoir.
The Anchor Inn, Plungar.
Peacock Inn, Ye Olde Windmill Inn, Redmile.

CAMPING
Rutland Arms Inn, by Grantham Canal, north of Woolsthorpe by Belvoir.
Chequers Inn, Woolsthorpe by Belvoir.

BED & BREAKFAST
1, Rosey Row, Woolsthorpe by Belvoir.

TOURIST OFFICE
The Guildhall Centre.
St. Peters Hill,
Grantham,
Lincolnshire. NG31 6PZ
Tel. 01476-66444

DAY CHALLENGE WALKS

JOHN MERRILL'S WHITE PEAK CHALLENGE WALK— 25 MILES - Circular walk starting from Bakewell and involving 3,600 feet of ascent, while passing through typical Peak District scenery river valleys, gritstone moorlands and outcrops, and limestone dales and plateaux. Interlaced are many historical items and eight inns! Whilst the walk is a challenge to walk in a day about 10 hours there is no time limit. By the summer of 1994 more than 16,000 people have walked the route and raised more than £150,000 for charity. 40 pages 15 colour photographs 6 maps
ISBN 0 907496 77 6 £6.95 NEW ENLARGED EDITION 2009

JOHN MERRILL'S DARK PEAK CHALLENGE WALK— 24 MILES - A demanding circular walk starting from Hathersage and taking in Stanage Edge, Derwent Edge, Back Tor, Derwent Reservoir, Win Hill and Bamford. Involves 3,300 feet of ascent. A magnificent high level route in the Peak District! 32 pages 14 photographs 8 maps ISBN 0 907496 66 0 £5.95

THREE COUNTIES CHALLENGE WALK - 28 MILES - Starting Tittesworth Reservoir, you embark upon a tough mountainous challenge over the countryside straggling the borders of Cheshire, Staffordshire and Derbyshire in the Peak District; passing in the final stages Three Shire Heads. 32 pages. 8 maps. 12 photographs. ISBN 1 874754 15 2.   £5.95

PEAK DISTRICT END TO END WALKS—23 AND 24 MILES - John Merrill's two favourite long walks in the Peak District he has walked both more than 30 times! The Gritstone Edge walk 23 miles, is downhill along the eastern edge system. The Limestone Dale-walk 24 miles, is down the limestone dales from Buxton to Ashbourne. Both are the grandslam of Peak District beauty. 52 pages 21 photographs 16 maps ISBN 0 907496 39 3 £5.95

JOHN MERRILL'S NORTH YORKSHIRE MOORS CHALLENGE WALK— 24 MILES - A seaside bash! Circular walk from Goathland in the heart of the moors. The route combines moorland, river valley and coastal walking, using Robin Hood's Bay as the half-way point, and involves 2,000 feet of ascent. 32 pages 18 photographs 8 maps ISBN 0 907496 36 9 £5.95

JOHN MERRILL'S YORKSHIRE DALES CHALLENGE WALK—23 MILES - Circular walk starting from Kettlewell, in the heart of the Dales. The walk is a challenge to complete within twelve hours and involves 3,600 feet of ascent while encompassing the scenic variety to be found in the National Park mountains, moorlands, limestone country and dale walking. 32 pages 16 photographs 6 maps ISBN 0 907496 86 5 £4.95

THE LITTLE JOHN CHALLENGE WALK—28 MILES - Circular walk from Edwinstowe in Sherwood Forest, the heart of Robin Hood country. Slightly longer day challenge, but flat country passing through forest, meandering rivers, gorges and historical houses. A really superb walk. 32 pages 16 photographs 8 maps ISBN 0 907496 46 6 £4.95

JOHN MERRILL'S LAKELAND CHALLENGE WALK- 18 MILES - A tough 6,000 foot ascent of ten lakeland peaks in a circular wall from the Langdale valley, including the summit of Scafell Pike, the highest mountain in England. 32 pages 23 photographs 12 maps ISBN 0 907496 50 4 £5.95

JOHN MERRILL'S STAFFORDSHIRE MOORLANDS CHALLENGE WALK— 24 MILES - A rewarding circular walk from Oakamoor in the Churnet Valley involving 2,000 feet of ascent. The walk is the grandslam of the area and includes Froghall Wharf, the Weaver Hills, Ordley Dale, Alton, and Ousal Dale. 32 pages 18 photographs 8 maps ISBN 0 907496 67 9 £4.95

THE RUTLAND WATER CHALLENGE WALK - 24 miles walk around Rutland Water, the largest man made reservoir In Europe. 36 pages, 7 maps 17 photographs ISBN 0 907496 88 1 £4.95

THE MALVERN HILLS CHALLENGE WALK - 20 mile walk from Great Malvern circling and traversing the Malvern Hills - more than 3,000 feet of ascent. 32 pages. 12 colour photographs, 6 maps. ISBN 0 907496 95 4 £6.95

THE SALTERS WAY - 25 miles across Cheshire from Northwich, following old saltways to the Pennine Hills at Slatersford. A walk from the plains to the hills! 32 pages. 4 maps. 12 photographs. ISBN 0 907496 97 0 £5.95

JOHN MERRILL'S SNOWDONIA CHALLENGE WALK - a tough 27mile walk with approximately 5,000 feet of ascent - from the sea to the summit of Snowdon....and back! 40 pages. 6 maps. ISBN 0 907496 79 2   £4.95

THE CARNEDDAU CHALLENGE WALK by Tony Hill. A walk from sea level to the summit of the Carneddau Range in Snowdonia. 20 miles with 4,750 feet of ascent. ISBN 1 874754 46 2. 32 pages. 6 maps. 10 photographs. £3.95

CHARNWOOD FOREST CHALLENGE WALK. - 25 MILES - Starting from Bradgate Park the route takes you over rocky tors, past monastic ruins and through woodland back to Bradgate Park. A beautiful walk in northern Leicestershire. 32 pages. 8 maps. 12 photograpghs   ISBN 0 907496 64 4   £5.95

THE BELVOIR WITCHES CHALLENGE WALK - 25 MILES. A magnificent walk in the Vale of Belvoir along the Grantham Canal, woodland, and past Belvoir Castle, seeing the sites of where three 17th century witches resided before being burnt to death in Lincoln on March 11th. 1619.
ISBN 1 903627-59-1 . 48 pages. 6 maps. 10 Colour photographs. £6.95 NEW EDITION

THE MIDDLEWICH CHALLENGE - 22 MILES - A magnificent walk in the heart of Cheshire. In the form of a figure of eight the walk, with the attractive village of Church Minshull as the axis, follows the whole length of the Middlewich Canal - a branch on the Shropshire Union Canal linking it to the Trent & Mersey Canal. The scenery is stunning! ISBN 1 874754 62 3. 32 pages. 5 maps. 8 photogragns. £4.95

JENNIFER'S CHALLENGE WALK - 23 MILES - Used to raise money for the National Rhuematoid Arthritis Society. A circular walk from Longcliffe, Derbyshire to Brassington, Kniveton, Hognaston, Carsington Water, Middleton and Bonsall. A quite peaceful walk in unspoilt countryside. 60pages. 10 maps. 1-903627-58-3 £7.00

THE QUANTOCK WAY - 28 MILES. The way is a magnificent 28 mile walk from Taunton to Minehead via the Quantock Hills, Watchet and coastal path. There is an alternative route from the Quantocks to Minehead via the Breedon Hills. This handy book describes the route with instructions and maps and includes a full amenities guide. ISBN 1 874754 29 2. 40 pages. 8 maps. 12 photographs. £6.95

COMPO'S WAY - 38 MILES by Alan Hiley. This is a magnificent 38 mile walk from Hunter's Bar, Sheffield over the Peak District Moors and Summer Wine Country to Holmfirth and Sid's Cafe'. The book gives extensive history notes along the way as you cross a range of terrain from Parks and wooded valleys to the high desolate moors of the Peak District. ISBN 1 874754 73 X. 40 pages. 12 maps. 15 photographs. £5,95

THE SWEET PEA CHALLENGE WALK - 28 MILES by John. Merrill. Wem in North Shropshire, the birthplace of the Sweet Pea, is the start and finishing point of this challenging and rewarding walk. The route over "rocky" hills includes the Prees branch of the Llangollen Canal. Combined they make a 28 mile challenge in a picturesque and little walked area. ISBN 1 874754 49 7. 40 pages. 10 maps. 12 colour photos. £6.95

THE GLYDERAU CHALLENGE WALK by Tony Hill. The author his written the Carneddeau Challenge. This challenge is more demanding and is a traverse of the Glyderau from Capel Curig to Bethesda, visiting all the peaks in the range. Covering a distance of 15.5 miles with 6,500 feet of ascent, the route offers some of the best mountain walking in North Wales. ISBN 1 874754 78 0. 32 pages. 6 maps, 10 photographs. £3.95.

THE FOREST OF BOWLAND CHALLENGE WALK - 24 MILES Starting from Beacon Hill, the routes crosses remote moorland of the Forest of Bowland. En route are several historial features and unspoilt villages. A worthy edition to the John Merrill collection! ISBN 1 874754 55 1. 32 pages. 6 maps. 12 photographs. £6.95

THE LINCOLNSHIRE WOLDS - BLACK DEATH CHALLENGE WALK- 26 MILES from LOUTH. The route follows quiet and delightful paths around the Lincolnshire Wolds linking together nine deserted medieval villages, ravaged by the Black Plague. The walk is full of history through unspoilt scenery which will come as surprise to flat Lincolnshire! The walk is a challenge to complete in a day but can be completed over two days with an overnight stop at Donington On Bains - the only shop, inn and accommodation on the route. The successful can obtain a special badge and certificate. 40 pages. sketches & photograpghs. ISBN 1-903627-19-2 £5.95

THE HAPPY HIKER CHALLENGE WALK - 24 MILES - A new walk in the White Peak, from Over Haddon - 25 MILES. 40 pages. 8 maps. 10 photographs. ISBN 1-903627 29 XNEW £5.95

THE EPPING FOREST CHALLENGE WALK - 21 MILES - Starting from the historic Waltham Abbey the walk takes in this impressive forest with views to London, 10 miles away. 40 pages. 12 photos. ISBN 9780955369100. £6.95.

Certificates, T shirts, and embroidered badges are available to all people who have successfully completed one of the challenge walks. So far more than £762,000 has been raised for charity by people doing these walks.

Follow the Countryside Code.

* Be safe - plan ahead and follow any signs.

* Leave gates and property as you find them.

* Protect plants and animals, and take your litter home.

* Keep dogs under close control.

* Consider other people.

EQUIPMENT NOTES
.....some personal thoughts from John N. Merrill

Today there is a bewildering variety of walking gear, much is superfluous to general walking in Britain. As a basic observation, people over dress for the outdoors. Basically equipment should be serviceable and do the task. I don't approve of or use walking poles; humans were built to walk with two legs! The following are some of my throughts gathered from my walking experiences.

BOOTS - For summer use and day walking I wear lightweight boots. For high mountains and longer trips I prefer a good quality boot with a full leather upper, of medium weight, with a vibram sole. I always add a foam cushioned insole to help cushion the base of my feet. Contary to popular belief, I do not use nor recommend Merrell footwear!

SOCKS - I generally wear two thick pairs as this helps minimise blisters. The inner pair are of loop stitch variety and approximately 80% wool. The outer are a thick rib pair of approximately 80% wool.

CLOTHES & WATERPROOFS - for general walking I wear a T shirt or cotton shirt with a cotton wind jacket on top, and shorts - even in snow! You generate heat as you walk and I prefer to layer my clothes to avoid getting too hot. Depending on the season will dictate how many layers you wear. In soft rain I just use my wind jacket for I know it quickly dries out. In heavy or consistant rain I slip on a poncho, which covers my pack and allows air to circulate, while keeping dry. Only in extreme conditions will I don overtrousers, much preferring to get wet and feel comfortable. I never wear gaiters, except when cross country skiing, in snow and glacier crossings.

FOOD - as I walk I carry bars of chocolate, for they provide instant energy and are light to carry. In winter a flask of hot coffee is welcome. I never carry water and find no hardship from not doing so, but this is a personal matter! From experience I find the more I drink the more I want and sweat. You should always carry some extra food such as trail mix & candy bars etc., for emergencies.

RUCKSACKS - for day walking I use a climbing rucksack of about 30/40 litre capacity and although it leaves excess space it does mean that the sac is well padded, with an internal frame and padded shoulder straps. Inside apart from the basics for one day, in winter I carry gloves, wear a hat and carry a spare pullover and a pair of socks.

MAP & COMPASS - when I am walking I always have the relevant map - preferably 1:25,000 scale - open in my hand. This enables me to constantly check that I am walking the right way. In case of bad weather I carry a compass, which once mastered gives you complete confidence in thick cloud or mist - you should always know where you are.

39

MY WALKING PHILOSOPHY
by John N. Merrill

I basically break many of the "accepted" rules of walking, but I believe my technique and approach has brought my walking to a higher level. Walking to me, is not physical fitness but having the right mental approach to the task. All you need is a strong faith and belief. I never consult with anyone or do any research beforehand. All this spoils the experience and "programmes" your mind to what is around the corner. I prefer not to know and discover as I go, this way making a greater impression on me. On a major walk at the end of each day, I run through the next day's stage on the map, so that on setting off the next day I am already programmed as to my day's destination. It is immaterial how far, how much ascent and descent, the day's destination is the key. I do not tick of the miles as I go for this makes the day go slowly and pulls you down mentally. On hills I adopt a steady pace and ascend, never stopping. If you stop on the way this too pulls you down mentally making the ascent seem long. During the day I basically don't stop for anything between 6 and 12 hours, just maintaining a steady comfortable pace. At the end of the day I have still enough energy and determination to carry on. To stop and restart part way through the day, means walking a couple of miles before I am in the "groove" again.

To many walking the Pennine Way is the ultimate walk, but after reaching Kirk Yetholm with 280 miles walked, you have hardly begun! By the time you have done that distance you have passed through the early stages of adjusting to your new way of life. The rucksack has become more bearable, the blisters have gone and your fitness has soared. But you need to walk 500 miles before you are settled into the task and have comfy feet. After 1,000 miles you are really adjusted and by 1,500 miles you can push yourself relentlessly. By 2,000 miles of continuous walking you are at your peak performance, but after 2,500 miles you are physically declining. You can reach your peak later by doing a reduced daily mileage but by 3,500 miles you are declining and by 4,000 miles I have usually lost 52 pounds in weight and struggling to walk well each day.

I always walk alone, so I can walk at my own pace. If you walk with others on a long walk if their pace is not compatible to yours you are more tired than they at the end of the day. Also you talk a lot which lessens the impact of the scenery and places on the way and you miss seeing the wildlife. I carry no mobile phone nor use poles. I usually wear T shirt and shorts but obviously warmer clothes in mountains and snow. In the pursuit of corporate money, the public are "brain washed" to stay in contact and drink water; they want the sales! I carry no water and don't usually drink during the day for anything upto 8 or ten hours. This is no hardship even when walking across the Mohave desert in 120° F. Once you start to drink you want more and the more you drink the more you sweat. Buddhist monks take this approach and have never come to any harm. My spiritual teaching as a Toaist Buddhist, concurs with their throught and training. You can live for four days without water and forty days without food. An injured walker in the Lake District survived for three weeks in gully, drinking a regular drip of water, until he was eventually found by a rescue party.

Infact US Military studies on thirst, while desert walking, in World War II found that -

> in 80° F heat a man can comfortably walk 45 miles without water.
> in 100° F heat, 15 miles
> in 120° F heat, 7 miles before collapsing.

Interestingly they found that walking 20 miles in the desert night, they recommended carrying 4 litres of water. During the day this increased to 8 litres.

Walking is the only way to fully appreciate the earth and you see it on its own terms.

OTHER JOHN MERRILL WALK BOOKS

CIRCULAR WALK GUIDES -
SHORT CIRCULAR WALKS IN THE PEAK DISTRICT - Vol. 1,2, 3 and 9
CIRCULAR WALKS IN WESTERN PEAKLAND
SHORT CIRCULAR WALKS IN THE STAFFORDSHIRE MOORLANDS
SHORT CIRCULAR WALKS - TOWNS & VILLAGES OF THE PEAK DISTRICT
SHORT CIRCULAR WALKS AROUND MATLOCK
SHORT CIRCULAR WALKS IN "PEAK PRACTICE COUNTRY."
SHORT CIRCULAR WALKS IN THE DUKERIES
SHORT CIRCULAR WALKS IN SOUTH YORKSHIRE
SHORT CIRCULAR WALKS IN SOUTH DERBYSHIRE
SHORT CIRCULAR WALKS AROUND BUXTON
SHORT CIRCULAR WALKS AROUND WIRKSWORTH
SHORT CIRCULAR WALKS IN THE HOPE VALLEY
40 SHORT CIRCULAR WALKS IN THE PEAK DISTRICT
CIRCULAR WALKS ON KINDER & BLEAKLOW
SHORT CIRCULAR WALKS IN SOUTH NOTTINGHAMSHIRE
SHORT CIRCULAR WALKS IN CHESHIRE
SHORT CIRCULAR WALKS IN WEST YORKSHIRE
WHITE PEAK DISTRICT AIRCRAFT WRECKS
CIRCULAR WALKS IN THE DERBYSHIRE DALES
SHORT CIRCULAR WALKS FROM BAKEWELL
SHORT CIRCULAR WALKS IN LATHKILL DALE
CIRCULAR WALKS IN THE WHITE PEAK
SHORT CIRCULAR WALKS IN EAST DEVON
SHORT CIRCULAR WALKS AROUND HARROGATE
SHORT CIRCULAR WALKS IN CHARNWOOD FOREST
SHORT CIRCULAR WALKS AROUND CHESTERFIELD
SHORT CIRCULAR WALKS IN THE YORKS DALES - Vol 1 - Southern area
SHORT CIRCULAR WALKS IN THE AMBER VALLEY (Derbyshire)
SHORT CIRCULAR WALKS IN THE LAKE DISTRICT
SHORT CIRCULAR WALKS IN THE NORTH YORKSHIRE MOORS
SHORT CIRCULAR WALKS IN EAST STAFFORDSHIRE
LONG CIRCULAR WALKS IN THE PEAK DISTRICT - Vol.1, 2 , 3, 4 and 5.
DARK PEAK AIRCRAFT WRECK WALKS
LONG CIRCULAR WALKS IN THE STAFFORDSHIRE MOORLANDS
LONG CIRCULAR WALKS IN CHESHIRE
WALKING THE TISSINGTON TRAIL
WALKING THE HIGH PEAK TRAIL
WALKING THE MONSAL TRAIL & SETT VALLEY TRAILS
PEAK DISTRICT WALKING - TEN "TEN MILER'S" - Vol One and Two
CLIMB THE PEAKS OF THE PEAK DISTRICT
PEAK DISTRICT WALK A MONTH Vols One, Two, Three, Four, Five & Six
TRAIN TO WALK Vol. One - The Hope Valley Line
DERBYSHIRE LOST VILLAGE WALKS -Vol One and Two.
CIRCULAR WALKS IN DOVEDALE AND THE MANIFOLD VALLEY
CIRCULAR WALKS AROUND GLOSSOP
WALKING THE LONGDENDALE TRAIL
WALKING THE UPPER DON TRAIL
SHORT CIRCULAR WALKS IN CANNOCK CHASE
CIRCULAR WALKS IN THE DERWENT VALLEY
WALKING THE TRAILS OF NORTH-EAST DERBYSHIRE
WALKING THE PENNINE BRIDLEWAY & CIRCULAR WALKS
SHORT CIRCULAR WALKS ON THE NEW RIVER & SOUTH-EAST HERTFORDSHIRE
SHORT CIRCULAR WALKS IN EPPING FOREST
WALKING THE STREETS OF LONDON
LONG CIRCULAR WALKS IN EASTERN HERTFORDSHIRE
LONG CIRCULAR WALKS IN WESTERN HERTFORDSHIRE
WALKS IN THE LONDON BOROUGH OF ENFIELD
WALKS IN THE LONDON BOROUGH OF BARNET
WALKS IN THE LONDON BOROUGH OF HARINGEY
WALK IN THE LONDON BOROUGH OF WALTHAM FOREST
SHORT CIRCULAR WALKS AROUND HERTFORD
THE BIG WALKS OF LONDON
SHORT CIRCULAR WALKS AROUND BISHOP'S STORTFORD
SHORT CIRCULAR WALKS AROUND EPPING DISTRICT
CIRCULAR WALKS IN THE BOROUGH OF BROXBOURNE

CANAL WALKS -
VOL 1 - DERBYSHIRE & NOTTINGHAMSHIRE
VOL 2 - CHESHIRE & STAFFORDSHIRE
VOL 3 - STAFFORDSHIRE
VOL 4 - THE CHESHIRE RING
VOL 5 - THE GRANTHAM CANAL
VOL 6 - SOUTH YORKSHIRE
VOL 7 - THE TRENT & MERSEY CANAL
VOL 8 - WALKING THE DERBY CANAL RING
VOL 9 - WALKING THE LLANGOLLEN CANAL
VOL 10 - CIRCULAR WALKS ON THE CHESTERFIELD CANAL
VOL 11 - CIRCULAR WALKS ON THE CROMFORD CANAL
Vol.13 - SHORT CIRCULAR WALKS ON THE RIVER LEE NAVIGATION -Vol. 1 - North
Vol. 14 - SHORT CIRCULAR WALKS ON THE RIVER STORT NAVIGATION
Vol.15 - SHORT CIRCULAR WALKS ON THE RIVER LEE NAVIGATION - Vol. 2 - South
Vol. 16 - WALKING THE CANALS OF LONDON
Vol 17 - WALKING THE RIVER LEE NAVIGATION
Vol. 20 - SHORT CIRCULAR WALKS IN THE COLNE VALLEY
Vol 21 - THE BLACKWATER & CHELMER NAVIGATION - End to End.

JOHN MERRILL DAY CHALLENGE WALKS -
WHITE PEAK CHALLENGE WALK
THE HAPPY HIKER - WHITE PEAK - CHALLENGE WALK No.2
DARK PEAK CHALLENGE WALK
PEAK DISTRICT END TO END WALKS
STAFFORDSHIRE MOORLANDS CHALLENGE WALK

For a free complete catalogue of John Merrill walk Guides send a SAE to The John Merrill Foundation

Visit our website - www.johnmerrillwalkguides.com

42

THE LITTLE JOHN CHALLENGE WALK
YORKSHIRE DALES CHALLENGE WALK
NORTH YORKSHIRE MOORS CHALLENGE WALK
LAKELAND CHALLENGE WALK
THE RUTLAND WATER CHALLENGE WALK
MALVERN HILLS CHALLENGE WALK
THE SALTER'S WAY
THE SNOWDON CHALLENGE
CHARNWOOD FOREST CHALLENGE WALK
THREE COUNTIES CHALLENGE WALK (PEAK DISTRICT).
CAL-DER-WENT WALK by Geoffrey Carr,
THE QUANTOCK WAY
BELVOIR WITCHES CHALLENGE WALK
THE CARNEDDAU CHALLENGE WALK
THE SWEET PEA CHALLENGE WALK
THE LINCOLNSHIRE WOLDS - BLACK DEATH - CHALLENGE WALK
JENNIFER'S CHALLENGE WALK
THE EPPING FOREST CHALLENGE WALK
THE THREE BOROUGH CHALLENGE WALK - NORTH LONDON

INSTRUCTION & RECORD -
HIKE TO BE FIT......STROLLING WITH JOHN
THE JOHN MERRILL WALK RECORD BOOK
HIKE THE WORLD - John Merrill's guide to Walking & Backpacking.

MULTIPLE DAY WALKS -
THE RIVERS'S WAY
PEAK DISTRICT: HIGH LEVEL ROUTE
PEAK DISTRICT MARATHONS
THE LIMEY WAY
THE PEAKLAND WAY
COMPO'S WAY by Alan Hiley
THE BRIGHTON WAY by Norman Willis

THE PILGRIM WALKS SERIES -
THE WALSINGHAM WAY - Ely to Walsingham - 72 miles
THE WALSINGHAM WAY - Kings Lynn to Walsingham - 35 miles
TURN LEFT AT GRANJA DE LA MORERUELA - 700 miles
NORTH TO SANTIAGO DE COMPOSTELA, VIA FATIMA - 650 miles
ST. OLAV'S WAY - Oslo to Trondheim - 400 miles
ST. WINEFRIDE'S WAY - St. Asaph to Holywell
ST. ALBANS WAY - Waltham Abbey to St. Albans - 26 miles
ST. KENELM TRAIL by John Price - Clent Hills to Winchcombe - 60 miles
DERBYSHIRE PILGRIMAGES
LONDON TO CANTERBURY- 75 MILES
LONDON TO ST. ALBANS - 36 MILES
LONDON TO WALSINGHAM - 194 MILES
FOLKESTONE, HYTHE TO CANTERBURY - 25 MILES
THE JOHN SCHORNE PEREGRINATIONS - 27 MILES by M. Mooney
ST CEDD'S PILGRIMAGE WALK - 24 MILES
ST BIRINIUS PILGRIMAGE WALK - 26 MILES

COAST WALKS & NATIONAL TRAILS -
ISLE OF WIGHT COAST PATH
PEMBROKESHIRE COAST PATH
THE CLEVELAND WAY
WALKING ANGELSEY'S COASTLINE.
WALKING THE COASTLINE OF THE CHANNEL ISLANDS
THE ISLE OF MAN COASTAL PATH - "The Way of the Gull."
A WALK AROUND HAYLING ISLAND
A WALK AROUND THE ISLE OF SHEPPEY
A WALK AROUND THE ISLE OF JERSEY
WALKING AROUND THE ISLANDS OF ESSEX

DERBYSHIRE & PEAK DISTRICT HISTORICAL GUIDES -
A TO Z GUIDE OF THE PEAK DISTRICT
DERBYSHIRE INNS - AN A TO Z GUIDE
HALLS AND CASTLES OF THE PEAK DISTRICT & DERBYSHIRE
TOURING THE PEAK DISTRICT & DERBYSHIRE BY CAR
DERBYSHIRE FOLKLORE
PUNISHMENT IN DERBYSHIRE
CUSTOMS OF THE PEAK DISTRICT & DERBYSHIRE
WINSTER - A SOUVENIR GUIDE
ARKWRIGHT OF CROMFORD
LEGENDS OF DERBYSHIRE
DERBYSHIRE FACTS & RECORDS
TALES FROM THE MINES by Geoffrey Carr
PEAK DISTRICT PLACE NAMES by Martin Spray
DERBYSHIRE THROUGH THE AGES - Vol 1 -DERBYSHIRE IN PREHISTORIC TIMES
SIR JOSEPH PAXTON
FLORENCE NIGHTINGALE
JOHN SMEDLEY
BONNIE PRINCE CHARLIE & 20 MILE WALK.
THE STORY OF THE EARLS AND DUKES OF DEVONSHIRE

JOHN MERRILL'S MAJOR WALKS -
TURN RIGHT AT LAND'S END
WITH MUSTARD ON MY BACK
TURN RIGHT AT DEATH VALLEY
EMERALD COAST WALK
I CHOSE TO WALK - Why I walk etc.
A WALK IN OHIO - 1,310 miles around the Buckeye Trail.

SKETCH BOOKS -
SKETCHES OF THE PEAK DISTRICT

COLOUR BOOK:-
THE PEAK DISTRICT.......SOMETHING TO REMEMBER HER BY.

OVERSEAS GUIDES -
HIKING IN NEW MEXICO - Vol I - The Sandia and Manzano Mountains.
Vol 2 - Hiking "Billy the Kid" Country. Vol 4 - N.W. area - " Hiking Indian Country."
"WALKING IN DRACULA COUNTRY" - Romania.
WALKING THE TRAILS OF THE HONG KONG ISLANDS.

VISITOR GUIDES - MATLOCK . BAKEWELL. ASHBOURNE.

Visit our website - www.pilgrimways.co.uk

For a free complete list of John Merrill walk Guides send a SAE to The John Merrill Foundation

Visit our website - www.johnmerrillwalkguides.com

43

BIRDS SEEN ON THE WALK -

I am indebted to Mike Haddrell, a keen walker and bird watcher, who walked the route over two days in early September 2010. He recorded seeing 34 different birds, which are listed below as he saw them, and reflect the variety of habitat that the walk passes through -

Wood pigeon	Green Spotted Woodpecker
Collared Dove	Buzzard
Robin	Magpie
Blue Tit	Pheasant
Rook	House Sparrow
Jackdaw	Chaffinch
Blackbird	Goldfinch
Mute Swan	Canada Goose
Moorhen	Kestrel
Mallard	Heron
Kingfisher	Great Tit
Coot	Wren
Tufted Duck	Reed Bunting
Great Crested Grebe	Greenfinch
Carrion Crow	Marsh Tit
Hedge Sparrow	
Starling	
Swallow	
House Martin	

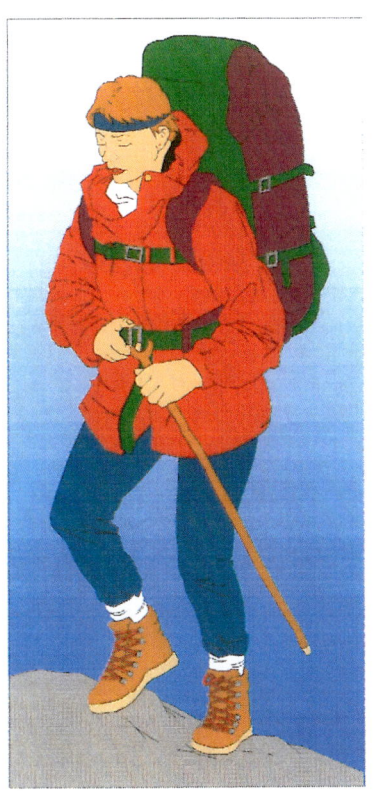

HOW TO DO A WALK

The walk in this book follows a public right of way, be it a footpath, bridleway, Boat or RUPP, which are marked in green lines on the Ordnance Survey 1:25,000 Explorer maps.

On each section I have detailed which map is needed and I would urge you to carry and use the map. As I walk I always have the map out on the section I am walking, constantly checking that I am walking the right way. Also when coming to any road or path junction, I can check on the map to ensure I take the right route.

Most the paths are signed and waymarked with coloured arrows but I would at best describe them as intermittent. They act as confirmation of the right of way you are walking and the arrow points in the direction of travel.

The countryside has the added problem of vandalism and you will find path logo's and Information Boards spray painted over and path signs pointing the wrong way! That is why I always advise carrying the map open on the area you are walking to check you are walking the right way. In my walking instructions I have given the name of each main and minor road, canal lock, and bridge, together with the house numbers where you turn and the name of inns passed. All to help you have a smooth and trouble free walk.

I confirm I have walked every route and written what I found at the time of walking.

These comments are not meant to put you off but to make you aware of some of the problems of walking in the countryside.

THE JOHN MERRILL MINISTRY

– Embracing & honouring all faiths.

John has been following his own spiritual path all his life, and is guided. He was brought up as a Christian and confirmed at the age of 13. He then went to a Quaker Boarding School for five years and developed his love for the countryside and walking. He became fascinated with Tibet and whilst retaining his Christian roots, became immersed in Buddhism. For four years he studied at the Tara Buddhist Centre in Derbyshire. He progressed into Daoism and currently attends the Chinese Buddhist Temple (Pure Land Tradition) in London. With his thirst for knowledge and discovery he paid attention to other faiths and appreciated their values. Late in life he decided it was time to reveal his spiritual beliefs and practices and discovered the Interfaith Seminary.

"When the pupil is ready, the teacher will appear". (Buddhist saying).

Here for two years he learnt in more depth the whole spectrum of faiths, including Jainism, Paganism, Mother Earth, Buddhism, Hinduism, Islam, Judaism, Sikhism, Celtic Worship and Shamanism. This is an ongoing exploration without end. He embraces all faiths, for all have a beauty of their own. All paths/faiths lead to one goal/truth. On July 17th. 2010 he was Ordained as an Interfaith Minister.

*"May you go in peace, with joy in your heart
and may the divine be always at your side."*

Using his knowledge and experience he combines many faiths into a simple, caring and devoted services, individually made for each specific occasion, with dignity and honour. He conducts special Ceremonies -

* Funerals   * Weddings   *Civil Partnerships   * Baby Blessings & Naming
* Rites of Passage   * Healing Ceremonies   * Pilgimages   * Inspirational Talks

For further information Contact John on -
Tel/Fax: 01992 - 762776
Email - marathonhiker@aol.com
Ministry site -www.pilgrimways.co.uk

*For more infomation about Interfaith work see -
www.interfaithfoundation.org*

Revd. John N. Merrill, HonMUni, R.I.M.A.
32, Holmesdale, Waltham Cross, Hertfordshire EN8 8QY

As I walk ....

I am not aware of my feet touching the earth, but am always looking ahead surveying the ground and intuitively place my feet where necessary. I look at all my surroundings, the hedges, trees, flowers and stop and observe the birds and animals that cross my path.

I see the wren calling in the hedgerows. I see the wild flowers growing throughout the seasons. I hear the call of a green woodpecker that sweeps ahead of me across the field. I near a scratching squirrel and call to it and watch him watching me briefly, before running and leaping effortless to a tree and up its bark. I follow and watch him hiding and ascending the tree, before swinging off onto another tree branch. I surprise a pheasant, who surprises us both and shrieks taking to the air urgently. I stop and admire a bee orchid growing alone on the field edge, knowing it is rare and must not be picked, for it will die.

I follow the path down to a brook and cross the footbridge and stop and gaze at the water to see if anything moves here or along the banks. Sometimes I see a fish, a water vole and occasionally a kingfisher - a mere flash of blue, but nevertheless a wondrous sight. I walk further and as I round a bend in the path in woodland, I surprise six roe deer who prick their ears, snort, and run away only to stop moments later to look again at this intruder in their world.

I marvel at these sights and sounds, which make me both joyful and humble at seeing the living unspoilt world, of which we all connected.

I walk beside a barbed wire fence and notice the sheep's wool caught on the barbs, as they either squeezed through or reached for a succulent piece of grass.

I watch the trees sway in the light breeze, the leaves flutter gently. I gaze at the fluffy clouds that glide across the sky. I walk in the cool damp air, but all is enjoyable and serene. Then suddenly the sun appears, and for a brief moment, illuminates my world and can see everything in its vibrant colours. As though showing me what is there and be patient. The clouds roll in and I am left with the magic of those priceless seconds. My heart is full of love for sharing this moment.

I walk on just looking and admiring all that my eyes see. I know I am guided and watched over, for I never put a foot wrong. I just walk with no preconceived ideas and no expectations. I just let it all happened in its own good time, which makes me very blessed at what has occurred.

I visit a church and are humbled at the workmanship and the story of the woodwork, stone and memorials. I touch the font and feel its story and energy.

As I walk though woodland and stop and rest by an oak tree and feel its trunk against my back. I feel its energy and wisdom, and say a prayer and touch it gently with my hand.

As I near the end of the walk I turn and raise my hand and say good-bye and thanks for allowing me to visit and enjoy your surroundings. It has meant much and I shall return to explore further and watch the unfolding kaleidoscope of life that exists there.

I walk and give thanks that I am able to do so with my body and mind. It is all a deep and profound experience without end.

© John Merrill - 9/2/2010